This sweet book belongs to:
SALLY
SWEET Treats

Life is short but Sweet
Sweet Tart

TRICK OR TREAT
girl power

13
GOOD
EVIL
Hotrod Honey

CUPCAKE
MANIAC
ADDICTED
DEATH

EVIL
DOLL

TOO SWEET 4 U

SWEET
SASSY
TRICK
or
?

LIVE FAST DIE YUM

candy
LIFE IS SWEET

SWEET TART
CUTE AS A CUPCAKE

HOT
Cherry
Pie
Cutie
PIE
NICE
NOT
NAUGHTY

SUGAR
DEATH
BEFORE
DIET

BITE ME
Beauty, Brains, Cupcakes

I ♡ CUPCAKES

HOT
Sweet as Hell

Delicious
SUGAR

MISS KITTY CUPCAKE

SWEET

13

CHEF
JUST MARRIED
Live to Bake

eye candy

COME IN FOR A BITE
BOO-TIFUL

RIP
LUV

13
YUM

Love Hurts
SWEET

what a ghoul wants...

WICKED
BITE
ME

EAT DRINK BE SCARY

BOO!
BH
HALLOWEEN

RIP

BOO!

cherry bomb
13
sweet

Made in the USA
Las Vegas, NV
09 May 2024

89757889R00044